To:

From:

7 Reasons to be Grateful You're a

single mom

Karen Sjoblom

New Leaf Press
A Division of New Leaf Publishing Group

7 Reasons to be Grateful You're a Single Mom

First Printing: December 2006

Copyright © 2006 by Karen Sjoblom. All rights reserved. No part of this book may be used or reproduced in any manner whatsoever without written permission of the publisher except in the case of brief quotations in articles and reviews. For information write: New Leaf Press, Inc., P.O. Box 726, Green Forest, AR 72638.

ISBN-13: 978-0-89221-653-6
ISBN-10: 0-89221-653-0
Library of Congress Catalog Number: 2006937328

Cover and Interior Design: LeftCoast Design, Portland, OR 97219
Printed in Italy

For information regarding author interviews, please contact the publicity department at (870) 438-5288.

Please visit our website for other great titles:
www.newleafpress.net

table of contents

F riendship makes prosperity more shining and
lessens adversity by dividing and sharing it.

Cicero, On Friendship, 44 B.C.

To all our friends who divide, and share, and shine...

K&E

CHAPTER 1

Gratefulness

means we get a

do-over day

You are going to make mistakes in this life,

so make sure you make good mistakes.

Erwin McManus

Seizing Your Divine Moment

hoever said the twos were terrible must never have stuck around for the threes—The Year of The Other. I don't know exactly when my darling angel turned into the devil's spawn, but it was ugly—full of petulance and tantrums, howling and defiance.

I had one nerve left, and Emma bungeed from it at every opportunity.

One day, I'd had a discouraging time at work, and from the moment I picked Emma up from daycare, she moaned and kvetched, but it was the whiny, tear-free kind of crying that sounds like hail on tin and makes your pulse actually audible in your ears. While we were driving on a busy highway, she struggled to get out of her carseat straps. I told her to put them back on. She glared at me and pulled the straps off completely, eyes blazing, chin jutting. And then it happened: I turned into my mother.

... it was the whiny, tear-free kind of crying that sounds like hail on tin and makes your pulse actually audible in your ears ...

Don't make me stop this car.

I pulled off on a side street, flung the van into park and stomped over to the passenger side rear door. I have no idea what came over me, but it was loud and possessed: I slid open the door and got about an inch from her face and yelled, "AAAAAUUUUU-UGH!" at the top of my voice.

If I remember correctly, I think her hair actually blew back a bit from the force.

Emma, wide-eyed, burst into tears, *real* tears this time, so saddened to discover her mother was a lunatic. I followed suit, and we both sobbed all the way home.

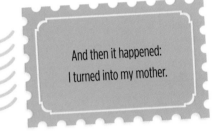

And then it happened:
I turned into my mother.

Of course, I apologized prolifically then, and Emma and I laugh about it now, but that episode remains my most un-fine moment in parenting. There are times when I have completely lost it—no patience, no logic, no nothing left. Usually, I give myself a time-out, but that day I was spent: the move, the divorce, the three-year-old, and the exhaustion had put me over the edge.

I think this is where grace enters in. As I understand it, *forgiveness* entails not getting what you deserve; *grace* entails not deserving what you get. I didn't deserve God's or Emma's grace that day, but it washed over me like a cool breeze. As moms, we're going to make huge mistakes at times, and yet, regularly, we get another chance.

Gratefully, three-year-olds have limited memories, and Emma can forgive and offer a taste of God's unending grace even when it feels like I can't—or shouldn't—forgive myself. I've had more times than I care to recall when we both go to bed at 7:30 pm and just surrender the day, knowing we get another chance—fresh slate, fresh grace—tomorrow.

CHAPTER 2

Gratefulness

says a sense of humor is

the best medicine

It feels like I'm babysitting

in the Twilight Zone.

Anne Lamott

Operating Instructions

On my last birthday, which was a biggie, Emma and I went to the mall so I could buy some perfume. I'd talked with the saleswoman before; she'd known I was looking for a certain scent. Pleasantly, she asked, "Who's this little girl?" I replied, "This is my daughter, Emma," who then smiled shyly. The saleswoman asked if Em wanted a

little spritz of perfume, too. As she sprayed some lily-of-the-valley on the back of her hand, she continued, "I only asked because I heard you talk so kindly to her that I wondered whether you were her grandma."

I dropped my jaw.

"Oh, I hear mothers screech at their kids all the time in here," she said. I smiled and quipped, "Well, the night is still young . . . ." We laughed.

So although it appeared I was squandering my paltry Social Security check on my perfume and that Emma would have to eat kitty vittles until next month, I chose to throw my head back and laugh, because we all know the alternative.

(I also have to say this came fast on the heels of picking Emma up at daycare earlier, where she and her little girl-friends rushed the door when I arrived: "Miss Karen! Is it true you're really f-f-f-forty today?" These little darlings, all holding hands with their fresh skin and bright eyes, looked at me like Methuselah's crazy Aunt Midge.)

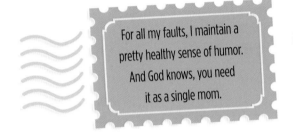

For all my faults, I maintain a pretty healthy sense of humor. And God knows, you need it as a single mom.

For all my faults, I maintain a pretty healthy sense of humor. And God knows, you need it as a single mom. Kids—and I say this with love—can wear the heck out of you. We simply cannot survive over the years with our edges intact. And I'm OK with my edges being worn down, as long as I can have a good laugh now and again.

Fortuitously, Emma is a riot, although she rarely knows how funny she is. She's getting to that age, though, where she rolls her eyes a lot and sighs *Mommmmm* when I've become the bane of her existence, which is regularly nowadays. But I can still get her pretty good and we just laugh our heads off. I'm Lucy; she's Ethel.

Last spring, we were looking at shepherd's hooks—the kind you stick in your garden to hold hanging planters. Emma didn't know what they were for, so I explained it to her, with this footnote: "And if your little friends are over, and someone gets all smarty pants on me, I can just go like this…" and I hooked my finger under Emma's collar and lifted up. Of course she was mortified —not only by the way my mind works, but because I laughed so hard at her reaction that I actually slapped my own thigh.

I think God makes our kids funny so we remember the good when the bad comes. But it's also one of those sweet, sweet things that makes all of it—even the eye-rolling—worthwhile.

CHAPTER 3

Gratefulness

means we are thankful that

God has a plan

Character is
both developed and
revealed by tests, and all of life is a
test. You are always being tested. God constantly
watches your response to people, problems, success,
conflict, illness, disappointment...You will be tested
by major changes, delayed promises, impossible
problems, unanswered prayers, undeserved
criticism and even senseless tragedies....

Rick Warren

The Purpose-Driven Life

Before I had a child, I found it amusing that people had to take multiple tests to get a driver's license but the same people could reproduce without *any* paperwork involved. So the irony of my attitude was not lost on me when I found myself at age 36, in the midst of a divorce, with two parenting evaluators in my home who were trying to determine whether I was fit to be Emma's mommy.

The afternoon visit had gone well; they'd just inspected Emma's room and were getting ready to leave when, in a moment that hadn't happened before or since, Emma's foot slipped on the carpet and she fell down the first half-flight of stairs, nearly taking out both women as she tumbled spread-eagle on the landing.

My interior mantra kicked in (don'tfreakoutdon'tfreakout don'tfreakout)

My interior mantra kicked in (*don'tfreakoutdon'tfreakoutdon't freakout*) as I stood over Emma and said calmly, "*That musta been scary.*" She nodded and took in a great gulp of air so she could wail. After a quick inspection, several *there-theres* and

many kisses, Em recovered nicely and I walked the women out the door. Emma then went back to her clay as though nothing unseemly had happened.

I walked into the kitchen and put my face in my hands.

OK, honey, let's go pack your bags. You're going to live with Daddy.

To this day, I have no idea why that episode happened or what it was supposed to mean. I'm willing to admit to overspiritualizing this, but perhaps God just wanted to get my attention, just wanted me to know He was still in charge. It was a frightening time for me—knowing the job I'd done every day more or less successfully was suspect. I no longer felt certain of my present or my future, and raising Emma was a huge part of that.

Five years later, I see God's hand in all of it. I see His timing, I see His help. I see that I've relaxed a lot since Emma took her little tumble. Certainly we've had our challenges, but we've got a nice little life going on here. We have purpose; we have peace. We have friends and family and support. I could not have fathomed this all those years ago; in spite of the

problems and the pain, I would do it all again.

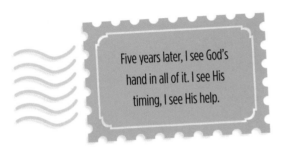

Five years later, I see God's hand in all of it. I see His timing, I see His help.

Perhaps most

importantly, I see

that I am not the

same scared

woman I was,

in the midst of this test. And I have to believe that was part

of God's plan all along.

CHAPTER 4

Gratefulness

means we are thankful

for the people in our lives

The experience of community
has taught me another lesson as well.
Not only must people who want to comfort
someone in pain make a decision to do so,
but people who need the comfort
must also decide to receive it.

Jerry Sittser

A Grace Disguised

A lot of times, God is verbose in His communication with me. At others, I get short commands: *Tell. Ask. Let.*

This has never been more apparent since I've divorced. I'm blessed with an amazingly easy child—just *one*—yet at times I've felt scared, exhausted, confused, overwhelmed. But

I've also been blessed with people, close and distant, who've entered our lives and changed us.

My usual *m.o.* calls for me to be stoic, self-sufficient, steely; in my vigor to need nothing and no one, I've not only pushed away but slapped the hands that shyly offered help to me. I'll never forget the drop-jawed reaction I gave my counselor when he said, "It's important we allow people to be inconvenienced on our behalf because it grows their faith and ours as well." I was stupefied.

But then I think of Christina, who brought us a four-course dinner just because she's been through moves with little kids and has watched them slobber and gnaw their chubby hands as you're unpacking instead of cooking. I think

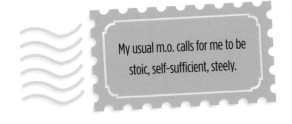

My usual m.o. calls for me to be stoic, self-sufficient, steely.

of my mom, who spent her vacation painting my heinous, dark brown kitchen cabinets. My own private financial planner *cum* coffee buddy, Alan, walked me through my shaky money situation and instructed me on life insurance and far more. My friend Kathy, in addition to a million other kindnesses, suffered along with me when a nasty reaction to an antibiotic caused me to throw up every two minutes; she stayed on the line when I called for help with Emma, then cut her off, threw up, called her back, cut her off, threw up. . . . Then she came over to hear that symphony in person. And my dear big brother, who called "just to check in and tell you I love you" minutes after I said to God, *I just can't do it; I don't have the juice to do another day.*

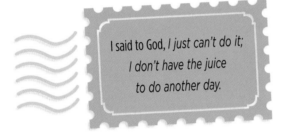

I said to God, *I just can't do it; I don't have the juice to do another day.*

At work, anonymous angels (and you know who you are), seeing me struggle on a part-time church salary and sporadic child support, listened and obeyed God's instructions: *Honey? Before you leave tonight, I want you to empty your wallet into Karen's mailbox. OK? And I'll be taking care of those little requests you made to Me . . . .* Several times I've opened my mail, found crumpled-up ones and fives with no note, gone into my office, and wept.

The tears that started in shame flow freer now, though, as God transforms me as a woman, as a mom: brokenness, connectedness, blessedness. It looks different than I thought, but it's beautiful nonetheless. *Tell. Ask. Let.*

CHAPTER 5

Gratefulness

means we thank God

for the job

Her face kissed by the sun
with charming freckles, two front teeth
missing, and eyes dancing with merriment,
who could refuse her? . . . She was a little girl
in her glory, unashamed in her desire to
delight, and be delighted in.

Stasi Eldredge

Captivating

As Emma and I were driving to a harvest party, she told me about a boy in her class who's giving her a hard time. "He told me I was ugly," she said.

So of course I feel my eyeballs about to explode, because this little snot has told my daughter this lie from the pit of hell, but I'm driving so I've got to keep calm. I said, "God has put really fabulous things in you, Emma. The

important thing is to know it in your head *and* in your heart. And if you've got it both places, you'll be OK." She said, "I know it up *here*," pointing to her forehead. "And you need to know it *here*," I said, tapping my heart. And I saw her in the rearview mirror, pantomiming picking something from her forehead and placing it over her heart.

I recognize the paradox of attempting to raise a daughter with a healthy self-image while her mom skulks through the world, trying to go unnoticed.

I myself rarely feel like a million bucks. I struggle, as most women do, with my image and worth. But God in His infinite wisdom gave me a daughter who believes, 98 percent of the time, that she's Royalty. She's so young and she *gets it*. I scratch my head, amazed, because often I am still so far from knowing, in my bones, my place in this world.

When I look at photos of myself as a child, I see a girl with a furrowed brow, trying to figure out how to do life. When I look at pictures of Emma, I see a tenderhearted angel who's plotting to live in a castle someday.

I recognize the paradox of attempting to raise a daughter with a healthy self-image while her mom skulks through the world, trying to go unnoticed. Perhaps God assigned Emma to me so I could reclaim that girl I once was—the one with the

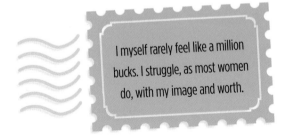

I myself rarely feel like a million bucks. I struggle, as most women do, with my image and worth.

bangs askew because she wouldn't sit still for a trim, the one

who gasped and clapped with delight

as she watched the snow fall,

dark and silent, during a

Chicago winter night.

So I chewed on this

while my Snow White and

I went trick-or-treating.

Everyone fussed and cooed over Emma, telling her what a beautiful princess she made. She said over her shoulder, "They think I'm beautiful." I replied, "You *are* beautiful." And she called back, "Well, of course I am," totally transparent and matter-of-fact.

The longer I'm a parent, the more I believe I can learn from Emma. Short of routines and safety, traditions and time, I think we as parents pretty much wind them up and watch them go. But there are times when I really *see* her and well up, saying a quiet *thank you* for the job.

CHAPTER
6

Gratefulness

means we thank God

for our strengths

and weaknesses

When I get honest,
I admit I am a bundle of
paradoxes. I believe and I doubt, I hope
and get discouraged, I love and I hate, I feel bad
about feeling good, I feel guilty about not feeling
guilty. I am trusting and suspicious. I am honest
and I still play games. Aristotle said I am a
rational animal; I say I am an angel with
an incredible capacity for beer.

Brennan Manning

The Ragamuffin Gospel

I am a very capable woman, except when it comes to jigsaw puzzles. It's embarrassing when your four-year-old is asking where Strawberry Shortcake goes and you can't help. I am spatially retarded—truly stunted when it comes to solving things visually. Perhaps I shouldn't operate heavy machinery either, but I digress.

When I had Emma, I had every intention of being the best mom in the whole world. I was going to cook and clean and be artsy and fun, right after I healed from the emergency C-section. She was home from the hospital about twelve minutes when I tried to pump some milk for her, because I decided it was time for her to eat a little something. Not fully understanding that I was physically incapable of producing real milk (it would be another day or so), I finished a long, drawn-out process with the pump in one hand and the phone in the other, getting coached by a La Leche League volunteer. I managed to squeeze out about half a teaspoon of *something*—my baby's nourishment!—and promptly spilled it all over the floor.

Sometimes my shortcomings haunt me; sometimes my strengths floor me. I am a woman who's fought like a wet cat for her kid, and I am a woman who's screamed like a crazy fishwife at the same. I'm a mom who's cleaned up buckets of vomit, and I'm a mom who's gotten queasy and pale when presented with a scrape. I want my daughter around forever, and I want two lousy hours to myself—*is that so much to ask?* I am both hero and coward, lighthearted and demanding.

I have no idea why God chose me to mother Emma, because I feel like such a *wreck* most of the time, but He did.

I've come to believe that, amazingly, I was hand-picked for this job. I long to be honorable and smart, silly and wise, beautiful and humble, and sometimes I pull that off. Other times, not so good. But I have to believe that she is mine, and I am hers, and as long as we're His—and

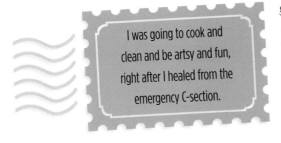

I was going to cook and clean and be artsy and fun, right after I healed from the emergency C-section.

I keep searching for Him—Emma will be fit to roam the world alone someday. In the meantime (and all of life as a single mom feels in the meantime), I try to do what I tell Emma to do: Show up. Try your best. Be kind. Share your stuff. Be willing to be wrong. And wear clean panties.

Gratefulness

means we thank God

for the journey

In the depths of every wound we
have survived is the strength we need to live.
The wisdom our wounds can offer us is a place
of refuge. Finding this is not for the faint
of heart. But then, neither is life.

Rachel Naomi Remen, M.D.

My Grandfather's Blessings

A kind and wise man in my life—a mentor, a rental dad—gave me a start when I was complaining about wanting to be "over" something in my life, as in, "Why aren't I over it already?" Smiling, he suggested it's not so much *over* as *through* and asked me what *it* is, because *it* will change. Regularly. He believes life has a low-level groaning to it, which surprises me because he's as peaceful a person as I've ever met. But around and throughout the groaning come moments of beauty, peace, thankfulness. Surprises, like *Well! Would you just look at that!* And we've got to hold it all lightly.

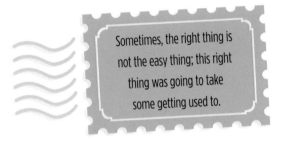

Sometimes, the right thing is not the easy thing; this right thing was going to take some getting used to.

It reminded me of when I was newly divorced—raw, musty, showing up but just barely.

I had packed up my girl and our stuff and had driven to the coast, hoping an afternoon on the beach would clear my head. At least, I thought, I'd be able to stare and breathe while Emma played in the sand.

There's something renewing about being by the water, and

I remember inhaling deeply, trying to wash away the confusion inside. Sometimes, the right thing is not the easy thing; this right thing was going to take some getting used to.

I watched Emma dig in, squealing, delighted. My heart leapt as it does sometimes, just watching her.

Fleece jacket, floppy hat and—oh!—those beautiful coppery-blonde baby curls, catching the light, she reminds me there's a God and He's on it. It was just what I needed: to breathe and watch.

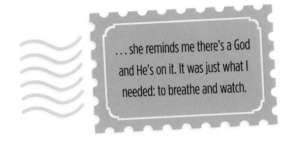

... she reminds me there's a God and He's on it. It was just what I needed: to breathe and watch.

It was a quiet day, Emma making her masterpieces and me sitting, watching. My sadness—my groaning—was pierced by the shriek of gulls, Emma's giggles, and the waves lolling. That silent space was filled; I didn't know gulls could be holy. We ate sandy peanut butter sandwiches and drank pink lemonade and it all was good.

Later in the day, Em's eyes at half-mast, ready to snooze all the way home, we packed up and I got a cup of coffee for the road: strong, hot, the way I like it. I said a quick prayer: If I could just hold these moments in my palm like I'd hold a baby bird, feeling the soft and the warmth and being content without having to *own* it . . . .

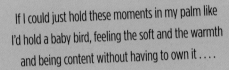

If I could just hold these moments in my palm like I'd hold a baby bird, feeling the soft and the warmth and being content without having to own it . . . .

"Mama, *look!*" Emma had scooped a fistful of sand, glittery, shimmering, and let it flutter through her fingers, saying *byebyebyebye*. I suddenly realized: She *gets* it, and I get *her*, and we both get Him. The rest will come out in the wash, eventually.

That day, it was enough to be on the road.

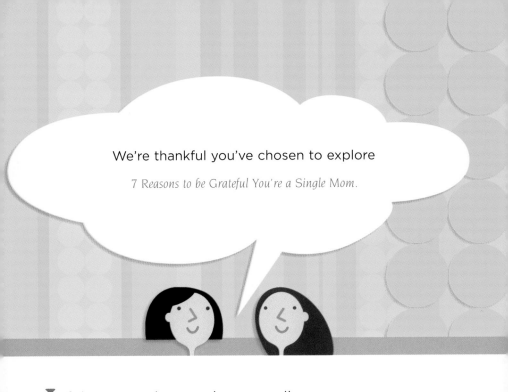

We're thankful you've chosen to explore

7 Reasons to be Grateful You're a Single Mom.

If these essays have made you recall your own

for-better-or-worse moments, take a few minutes

to write some thoughts to perhaps share with your

child(ren) sometime... like after they have their *own* kids.

How Many Do-Over Days Can We Have?

Sometimes during a long string of seemingly wasted days, we long for meaning, purpose, and some guarantee this child-rearing gig will turn out positively. Is there a time you can look back on, now from a different perspective, when the dreariness of day-to-day family duties produced a bit of hope after a long, dry spell?

When Your Sense of Humor is Buried Beneath Your Laundry...

Immediately following 9/11, New York Mayor Rudy Giuliani suggested we needed to find a way to laugh again—while we're still crying. Some might suggest this applies to motherhood as well. Can you recall some times when laughter gave way to tears . . . and tears gave way to laughter?

It's been said that life has to be lived forward, but can only be understood backward. As a mom, what experiences have you had that have shifted your view of your plans versus God's plans? In what areas are you still hoping your plans will win?

s Hillary Clinton noted, it takes a village to raise a child. Who are the members of your tribe, your people? How have they helped you raise your family? In what areas do you feel you *have* to go it alone?

It's a Tough Job, But Someone's Got to Do It...

Some say parenting is the only job for which we apply without a clue of what we're doing. Do you view parenting as a chore? A job? A gift? How has it been different from what you expected or hoped for?

o you feel hand-picked by God to parent your specific kids? Does this notion change your view of your own strengths and weaknesses?